HOMETOWN HISTORY
PORTSMOUTH

I'm Charles Dickens – did you guess? Read about me on page 23.

Admiral Lord Nelson at your service! You can find me on page 19.

JIM RIORDAN

HOMETOWN WORLD

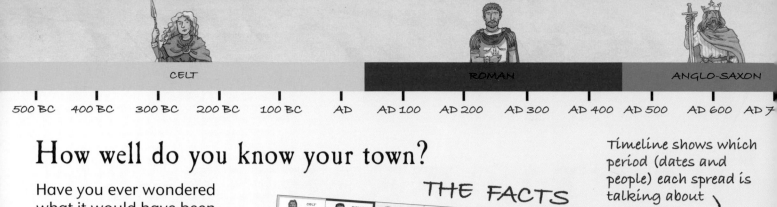
How well do you know your town?

Have you ever wondered what it would have been like living in Portsmouth when the Vikings arrived? How about standing next to Henry VIII, watching as the *Mary Rose* sank in the Solent? This book tells the story of your town, with all the important and exciting things that have happened there.

Want to hear the other good bits? A team of brainy people have worked on this book to make sure it's fun and informative. So what are you waiting for? Peel back the pages and be amazed at what happened in your town.

Timeline shows which period (dates and people) each spread is talking about

THE FACTS

Clear informative text

Hometown facts to amaze you!

'Spot this!' game with hints on something to find in your town

THE EVIDENCE

Go back in time to read what it was like for children growing up in Portsmouth

Exciting historical images

Each period in the book ends with a summary explaining how we know about the past

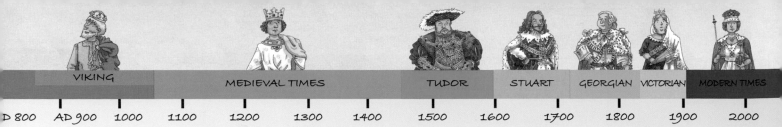

Contents

The Romans are Here!

It's another busy day at Portus Adurni. The Roman soldiers and their slaves are building their fort on the harbour. The soldiers mainly stand and watch, refusing to do any heavy work. Instead they stay on the lookout for pirates. A wooden crane is being used to lift big pieces of flint. A slave inside the crane's treadmill walks heavily to make the treadmill turn. Sweating, he watches as the stone lifts slowly off the ground. He pauses for a moment to watch the Roman soldiers on the brow of the hill, then carries on – he doesn't want to get into trouble again.

Portus Adurni

After invading Britain in AD 43 and conquering most of it, the Romans had to think about how they would defend it. Over 200 years later, they built a fort at Portus Adurni, which means 'port entrance'. It is believed that the Romans sent one of their best men – a naval commander called Carausius – to make the fort stronger and get rid of pirates. With Carausius in charge, Roman workmen built walls that were 3 metres thick and 6 metres high – that's taller than a double-decker bus! Portus Adurni is better known today as Portchester Castle.

Carausius then decided to make himself Emperor of Britain. After eight years he was killed by one of his own men, and the Romans ruled again. They built roads to two nearby camps: north to Winchester, and east to Chichester. The roads were straight and long-lasting, with several layers of stones and a ditch at either side to drain the water.

Most of the original walls at Portchester Castle are still standing today. They are the best example of Roman walls in Europe!

Greetings, Britons, I am the mighty Carausius. Check out my handsome face on this coin!

Life at the Fort

The Roman legionaries at Portus Adurni were in charge of local men and their families. Roman women and children also lived at the fort, with the soldiers. They ate meat from pigs, cows, sheep and deer, as well as fish and birds. They built ovens to bake bread and kept cats and dogs to hunt rats. The Romans also brought fruit and vegetables from Rome, such as grapes, cherries, apples, pears, onions, peas, radishes and celery.

Here are the two sides of a coin from when Carausius was ruling.

The original British name for the nearby Isle of Wight was 'Ynys-Wyth', meaning the 'channel island'. The Romans called it 'Vectis'.

Roughly 15,000 cartloads of flint were used to build the fort, carried from nearby Portsdown Hill.

About 1,000 men worked together to help build our fort.

The Landgate was a main entrance to the castle. The gate itself would have been much wider in Roman times.

Building Britain

People living in Britain at the time of the Roman invasion were called Britons. While local Britons lived in smoke-filled thatched huts, the Romans built houses made from bricks and tiles, with glass windows. The Romans taught people how to build houses and villas. They even had central heating under the floors, and charcoal stoves, so the rooms were free of smoke.

SPOT THIS!

Many people lived at Portchester castle after the Romans, including King Richard II. Can you spot this door to his palace?

...AD 293 CARAUSIUS IS KILLED...ABOUT AD 407 ROMAN ARMY LEAVES BRITAIN...

5

Fishbourne Palace, near Portsmouth, was the first large Roman house to be built in Britain. Here is an imaginary diary entry written by a British slave working in the gardens at Fishbourne.

These Romans certainly know how to get their five a day!

Some days I am lucky enough to enjoy my work. Today was one of them. Spring is finally here! The large garden at Fishbourne looks beautiful with all of its flowers and statues. But there is a lot of work to be done.

Our masters from Rome brought new plants when they arrived. It must be warm and sunny in Rome because not everything survives our frosts here. Their apples and pears grow quite well but their peach trees and grapevines are not so good.

My master asked me to plant something called onions. I am certain these onions contain magic. They bring tears to my eyes when I am peeling and cutting them – as if to punish me!

My master also sends goods abroad on galley ships rowed by slaves. Last week he loaded up bear and wolf skins, slaves and hunting dogs. Before that he sent out silver and iron. Sometimes I think I would like to sail on a galley ship. But where would I go? It is probably safer to stay in my gardens at Fishbourne…

This model shows how Fishbourne Palace would have looked in Roman times.

Fishbourne Palace contains the biggest collection of mosaics in Britain. This one shows Cupid, the Roman god of love and beauty, riding a dolphin.

Ships like this model would have carried grain and other goods from abroad into the harbour.

This small gold ring probably belonged to a woman or child. The oval gemstone shows a bird.

How do we know?

We can learn a lot about how the Romans lived from discoveries at Fishbourne Palace. The palace sat underground for hundreds of years until workmen laying water pipes found it in 1960. After months of digging, we learned that the site had started off as a military base at the time of the Roman invasion. By the end of the 1st century, it had grown into a wealthy palace. The mosaics are very useful as they often show the dates of the emperor ruling at that time.

Roman coins of the 3rd and 4th centuries have been found all over Portsmouth. Coins also show dates and names of emperors. Coins inside skulls were found at Portchester Castle and in a grave in a Paulsgrove chalk pit. The Romans put a coin under a dead person's tongue because they believed it helped look after the person's soul.

We know that women lived at Portchester Castle because accessories such as brooches and hairpins were found. Human bones have also been discovered there, and animal bones, which give us clues about what the Romans ate.

New Visitors

With the Romans gone, new tribes come to visit. Their colourful galleys sail around Vectis and then land at Portsmouth. The travellers unload their goods and look around. The air is mild, but the harbours are full of stinking mud when the tide goes out. Crops and cattle don't do well in the scrubland and forest. They ask themselves whether it is worth settling here. A few people stay to fish and farm on Portsea Island, but most move on to richer parts.

Portes Mutha

The first visitors after the Romans were probably Jutes from Jutland (now Denmark), followed by Angles from Angel in Denmark, and then Saxons from northern Germany.

The Anglo-Saxon Chronicle is a history of Anglo-Saxon England, handwritten in Old English by monks. One monk wrote: 'In 501, Port and his two sons, Bieda and Maegla, came to Britain in two ships at a place called Portes Mutha'. We do not know if this really was Portsmouth but it could have been the earliest mention of a port mouth. It is possible that this led to Portsmouth's name today. Many parts of the town still have Saxon names. For example, Milton means 'Middle Farm' or 'Middle Hamlet', Buckland means 'Charter Land' and Eastney means 'East of the Island'.

At that time, England was made up of three kingdoms. Northern England was called Northumbria, the Midlands were called Mercia and southern England was known as Wessex. Portsmouth was Wessex's main naval defence.

The Anglo-Saxon Chronicle, carefully handwritten by monks, shows Portsmouth recorded as 'Portes Mutha'.

...AD 501 PORTES MUTHA IS MENTIONED IN ANGLO-SAXON CHRONICLE...

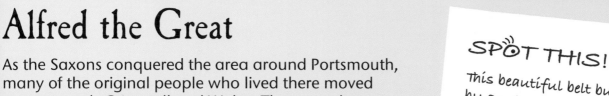
Alfred the Great

As the Saxons conquered the area around Portsmouth, many of the original people who lived there moved west towards Cornwall and Wales. They were known as Britons.

Saxon England used the 'Hundred' system. This meant that every hundred households had a court to look after them. The Portsmouth Hundred included Bocheland, Copenore, Cosseham, Frodintone and Wimerings. You might know these places better as Buckland, Copnor, Cosham, Fratton and Wimering.

The most famous Saxon was Alfred, who was king of Wessex for 28 years. His palace was just north of Portsmouth, at Winchester. Alfred built a navy of 100 ships to patrol the English Channel.

SPOT THIS!

This beautiful belt buckle was worn by an Anglo-Saxon warrior. You can see it at Curtis Museum in Alton, just north of Portsmouth.

The coasts of southern England were under constant attack from invaders throughout Saxon times. King Alfred became known as 'Alfred the Great' because his army defended England so well.

The Saxons used magic spells and lucky charms to try and keep diseases away. They wrote down their spells in letters called 'runes'.

Dear God, please invent some kind of machine so I don't have to write everything by hand.

Religion

The early Saxons were pagans, which means that they worshipped lots of different gods. In AD 597, Pope Gregory sent missionaries from Rome to persuade Saxons to abandon their pagan gods and worship one Christian God. It was during this time that great monasteries and abbeys were built, including around Portsmouth. These buildings became places of learning where monks made beautiful religious books, written and painted by hand.

People made their own entertainment in Anglo-Saxon Britain. Kings and lords often kept a jester, storyteller and musicians to amuse them in the huge halls of their palaces. Bands of minstrels roamed the country, looking for wealthy lords or thanes to pay for their music. Here is an imaginary letter from a young minstrel to his friend.

> This singing makes me thirsty. I could do with a good swig of mead!

Dear Wigbert,

I am travelling the land with my master. Our troupe of minstrels earns a living by entertaining lords with our drum, harp and pipe. I play both the horn and the pipes. My master plays the harp, which is harder to play.

Not long ago, I played for King Alfred in his palace at Winchester. There were also acrobats doing cartwheels and jugglers with balls and sticks. Even the King performed, reciting whole sections of a poem about a hero called Beowulf.

On our travels we eat whatever we can find in the woods – usually nuts, berries and roots. Sometimes we set traps for hare, deer and wild boar, though it is easier to catch wild duck and pheasants. At King Alfred's palace, I tasted pig roasted on a turnspit, washed down with a cup of mead. The mead was tasty but it made my head spin!

I am now on my way home. Our journey is dangerous as the forest is full of outlaws waiting to rob anyone who passes by. I hope to play some sea shanties with you soon!

Your friend,
Baldwulf

'Beowulf' is the oldest known poem in the English language. Here's the first page, written in Old English, the language used by the Saxons.

The Saxons lived in huts like these, with thatched roofs and wooden walls.

The Saxons gave Portchester its name. They seemed to misunderstand the Roman word 'castra', which means 'forts', and instead called any group of Roman buildings a 'caester'. Most Roman forts and towns now have the ending 'chester', 'caster' or 'cester', which are all versions of the original Saxon word.

The sea-side entrance to Portchester Castle is called the Watergate. It was originally built in late Saxon times.

A boss is a type of raised, rounded decoration, often found on shields or swords.

How do we know?

Recent digs in and around Portsmouth give us proof of early Saxons, such as Saxon pottery from the 5th to 6th century. Near the middle of Portchester Castle, a late Saxon hall was discovered.

In the late 1800s, workmen opened up two burial mounds on Portsdown Hill, finding the remains of 12 Saxon soldiers. One had a piece of iron embedded in his skull, suggesting that he had died in battle.

Another 33 Anglo-Saxon burials were discovered at Snell's Corner, near Horndean. They contained bronze and iron buckles, beads, rings and bronze ornaments. There was also a small drinking cup and a collection of weapons, including knives, spears and sword bosses.

Several kilometres away, 20 graves were found near Southwick Crossroads, containing 25-30 skeletons. Most of the remains were of adult males, suggesting that the site was near the scene of a battle, perhaps between British settlers and Saxon invaders.

CELT
500 BC

ROMAN
AD 43-410

ANGLO-
SAXON
AD 450-
1066

VIKING
AD 865-
1066

MEDIEVA
TIMES
1066-14

Viking Invaders

Raise the alarm! It's the Vikings! They cross the English Channel and make their way towards Portsmouth Harbour, their swords flashing in the sunlight. The wooden dragons at the bows of their ships rock up and down in the choppy water. But here come a hundred or more of King Alfred's ships, with men bearing swords and axes, and sails billowing in the wind. They soon scatter the Viking longboats and send some of them sinking beneath the waves. Long live King Alfred!

I order you to stop, sea!

King Canute

The Vikings, also known as the Norsemen or Danes, were a German tribe that had settled in Scandinavia. Between the 8th and 11th centuries they took over most of northern Europe. Although King Alfred defeated them in AD 897, more groups of Vikings continued to attack the Wessex shores. They finally managed to invade when King Ethelred 'the Unready' was on the throne. Ethelred's nickname comes from the Old English meaning 'bad plan' and suggests he received poor advice from his advisers.

In AD 998, the Vikings made their base on the Isle of Wight under Sven Forkbeard. Nearby villages, like Bishops Waltham, were destroyed. The Kingdom of Wessex finally surrendered and, in 1017, the Saxon council accepted Canute as the first Viking king of England.

Legend has it that King Canute ordered his men to carry him down to the sea on his throne. He spoke to the sea, telling the tides to stop rising. But when the sea did not stop moving, Canute explained to his men that God was the only true king, who commanded the heaven, earth and sea.

...AD 998 VIKINGS CAPTURE ENGLAND'S SOUTHERN SHORES...

A Warrior Race

The Vikings enjoyed watching horse races and sword fights, stone-throwing, wrestling and archery. In winter, families would huddle around fires to tell riddles and listen to stories and music. They especially loved stories about their gods and brave heroes who died in battle.

King Canute made his home on the shores at Bosham, just east of Portsmouth, taking taxes, called *Danegeld*, from the local people. By the time King Canute was on the throne, the Vikings had become Christians.

Viking helmets did not have horns. Horned helmets were awkward to wear and risked injury to warriors on the same side.

I want people to remember me as a great warrior.

SPOT THIS!

King Canute's daughter drowned when she was only eight years old. You can find a stone marking her grave behind the pulpit in Bosham Church. Her coffin is buried beneath.

This is Bosham Church, which contains the grave of King Canute's daughter. The tombstone says she died 'early in the 11th century'.

Some of our names for the days of the week come from Viking gods. Other Viking words include egg, skin, sky, knife and happy.

Harsh Punishment

Like the Saxons, the Vikings gave out cruel punishments. People accused of telling lies might have their tongues cut out. Anyone making fake coins would have a hand chopped off. To prove whether someone was guilty or not, the accused person might have to hold a piece of red-hot iron. The burned hand was then wrapped in bandages. After three days, the bandages were removed and if the hand had healed, the person was innocent. If not, they were guilty.

CELT
500 BC

ROMAN
AD 43-410

ANGLO-
SAXON
AD 450-
1066

VIKING
AD 865-
1066

MEDIEV
TIME.
1066-1

The Navy Comes to Town

It's that time of year again – the fair is in town! Portsmouth is filled with weavers, spinners, farmers and all kinds of other merchants, selling their goods. There is a circus too, with clowns, men on stilts, lions and bears. Apparently, there is even an elephant this year. Imagine that – a real live elephant on Portsmouth High Street! The town is buzzing with noise and excitement.

> How did I get stuck with babysitting duty? This is one giant baby!

Time to Trade

> The fair in Portsmouth was declared 'open' when an open hand, carved from wood, was displayed on the High Street.

In 1180, the new town of Portsmouth was created by a merchant and landowner called Jean de Gisors. It was built on wasteland. Before that, there had been villages in the area but not an actual town.

In 1194, King Richard the Lionheart granted Portsmouth a charter to hold a fair for a fortnight each year. He also allowed the town to hold a market every Thursday, bringing merchants and tradesmen to the town. King John – the brother of King Richard – used Portsmouth in 1205 to assemble a large army and fleet of ships for an attack on France.

...1180 THE NEW TOWN OF PORTSMOUTH IS CREATED BY JEAN DE GISORS...

 TUDOR 1485-1603	STUART 1603-1714	GEORGIAN 1714-1837	 VICTORIAN 1837-1901	 MODERN TIMES 1902-NOW

A Tudor Tower

The first of the Tudors, Henry VII, came to the throne in 1485. Both Henry VII and his son, Henry VIII, saw Portsmouth as an important place, investing lots of money in the town and the navy. In 1495 a square tower was built and an iron chain was put across the harbour entrance to keep out enemy ships. Henry VII also opened a dockyard with a special dry dock where ships could have their bottoms scraped clean and coated with tar.

Henry VIII ordered the wooden round tower at the harbour entrance to be rebuilt in stone. In 1544 he built a stone castle, now called Southsea Castle.

Southsea Castle was built for Henry VIII in 1544.

What England needs is a good, strong navy.

SPOT THIS!

Near to the Tudor Square Tower is the 'Bonds of Friendship' monument. Have you seen the real thing?

The Royal Navy

Henry VII had built merchant ships to take wool and wheat to France and Spain, bringing back wax, iron and wine. Since England was at peace, he had little need of warships. But his son had to fight the Scots and the French. So Henry VIII built great battleships to outrival France. He used Portsmouth as the meeting place for the English fleet and a base for attacking France. For this he is known as the 'founder of the Royal Navy', with Portsmouth as its home.

One of the king's best new ships was built and launched from Portsmouth. It was the *Mary Rose*, named after his younger sister. To the horror of the king and everyone watching, the *Mary Rose* and its crew sank accidentally in the Solent in 1545.

Elizabeth I invented the lottery!

That's the Ticket!

Elizabeth I launched Britain's first lottery in 1566. She would use the money made from ticket sales to repair harbours and for other general public purposes. About 400,000 tickets were on sale, costing 10 shillings each — equal to half a pound in Tudor money. A labourer or low-paid worker earned only five to ten pounds a year in Tudor times, so a lottery ticket wasn't cheap.

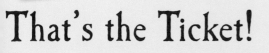

When the *Mary Rose* sank in the Solent in 1545, Henry VIII and many other people were watching. The imaginary account opposite comes from a sailor who saw the ship sinking.

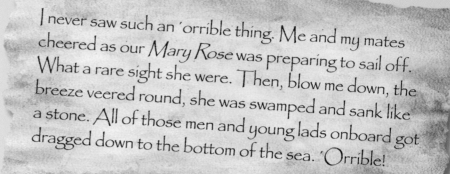

I never saw such an 'orrible thing. Me and my mates cheered as our *Mary Rose* was preparing to sail off. What a rare sight she were. Then, blow me down, the breeze veered round, she was swamped and sank like a stone. All of those men and young lads onboard got dragged down to the bottom of the sea. 'Orrible!

Nit combs were found in the wreck of the *Mary Rose*. If you look closely enough, you can still see the nits!

> This ship is absolutely jumping with head lice! At least I don't have to worry too much...

This is part of the Cowdray engraving, which shows the *Mary Rose* sinking. On the left, you can see the tops of two masts.

The top of one of the masts was found with the shipwreck.

This cannon was also saved from the shipwreck. The ship spent 437 years at the bottom of the sea!

The skeleton of a small dog was found with the Mary Rose. She has been named 'Hatch' by staff at the Mary Rose Museum.

Sailors on the Mary Rose must have liked playing backgammon.

How do we know?

The *Mary Rose* was discovered in 1971 and carefully lifted from the seabed in 1982. Many items were discovered along with the ship, which tell us lots about Tudor times and life at sea. As well as artefacts, we have ship logs, diaries and letters which all paint a picture of life at that time.

Henry VIII chose a man called John Leland to research and make records of local history. Leland travelled the country from 1540 to 1546. After visiting Portsmouth, he wrote: 'The toun of Portesmouth is bare and little occupied in time of pece... There is one fair striate in the town from west to north este. There is one...church.'

Famous diaries from visitors like Samuel Pepys and John Evelyn talk about Portsmouth during Stuart times. Reports, newsletters and pamphlets all describe events in Portsmouth during the Civil War (1642 to 1646). The First Earl of Clarendon described Portsmouth as 'the strongest and best fortified town then in the kingdom'.

17

Press Gang!

The local pub is small and cosy. A few men sit and talk, drinking warm ale from wooden tankards. The landlord suddenly looks up as a group of men walk by the dusty window. 'Press gang!' he shouts. 'Quick – hide!' As the door bursts open, the men inside panic. One man manages to duck around the corner to a secret hiding place, just in time. But for the others it is too late. They are the navy's new recruits – another successful night for the press gang.

Joining Up

Bad conditions on ships put off many men from becoming sailors. The Navy sent out gangs to force or 'press' young men to fill the fighting ships. They became known as 'press gangs'. Pub landlords sometimes had a secret staircase and 'cubby holes' behind the wooden walls for their customers to hide in. Once, the press gang arrived at the fair in Portsmouth. Unable to escape, some men quickly changed clothes with their girlfriends to avoid being caught!

How do I look, darling? I think this dress suits me. And I LOVE this hat!

Nelson

Horatio Nelson was born in Norfolk in 1758. He commanded several ships in the British navy, many of which would have sailed from Portsmouth. Launched in 1765, HMS *Victory* later became Admiral Lord Nelson's flagship.

On 14th September 1805, Nelson woke up at the George Inn in Portsmouth. He was about to set sail from Portsmouth in HMS *Victory* for the last time. Nelson had to sneak out of the back door of the inn to avoid the gathering crowds. But as he reached Southsea beach, Nelson was met by swarms of people cheering and wanting to shake his hand. Having lost one arm in battle, Nelson told the people that he wished he had two hands in order to greet more of them.

Sneaky press gangers would drop the king's shilling into a man's drink. The man had then accepted his first payment from the navy and had no choice but to join up.

Victory!

The Battle of Trafalgar took place in October 1805, with Britain fighting the French and Spanish. Following the lead of Nelson in HMS *Victory*, the British navy won. Three months later, HMS *Victory* returned to Portsmouth carrying Nelson's body. In the triumph of Trafalgar, Nelson was shot and died onboard his flagship, aged 46. HMS *Victory* returned to England and was finally docked at Portsmouth in 1812.

Around 6,000 trees were used to make HMS *Victory*!

Can you guess how Trafalgar Square got its name?

SPOT THIS!

As well as having a famous column in Trafalgar Square in London, Nelson has a statue in the centre of Portsmouth. Can you find it?

England expects!

British war hero Admiral Lord Horatio Nelson

How do we know?

Daniel Defoe, the author of *Robinson Crusoe*, came to Portsmouth in 1724. He wrote that Portsmouth had been chosen 'for the best security of the navy above all the places in Britain; the entrance into the harbour is safe, but very narrow, guarded on all sides by terrible platforms of cannon'.

Local newspapers from the time, such as the *Hampshire Chronicle* and the *Portsmouth Telegraph*, contain eyewitness accounts of the Battle of Trafalgar and Nelson's death in 1805.

HMS *Victory* is now docked in Portsmouth Harbour. Visitors can climb aboard to see how the Georgian navy lived and worked.

Holiday Time

What a beautiful day for a trip to the seaside! With money to spend, holidaymakers flock to sunny Southsea from the mills of the North and Midlands. They climb down from the new steam train at the Harbour Station. Almost straight away, they get their first view of the sea and busy dockyard, with HMS *Victory* peering past Semaphore Tower at them. They visit the thriving shops and markets and go for strolls along Clarence or South Parade piers.

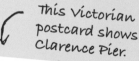

This Victorian postcard shows Clarence Pier.

A direct trainline from London to Portsmouth Harbour brought holidaymakers from all over the country.

Boom Town

Queen Victoria was on the throne from 1837 to 1901. During that time the British Empire grew to cover a fifth of the world. Small towns like Portsmouth grew into booming industrial centres. Portsmouth's population rose from 32,000 in 1801 to nearly 170,000 at the end of the century.

Ship building and repairing were in high demand, especially after ships changed from wooden sailing vessels to iron propeller-driven ships.

Such fast progress made a few people very wealthy but brought misery for many others who lived in poor conditions where diseases like cholera and typhus killed thousands.

...1837 VICTORIA BECOMES QUEEN...1843 SS GREAT BRITAIN IS LAUNCHED...

Brilliant Brunel

The great engineer Isambard Kingdom Brunel was born near Portsmouth's Dockyard in 1806. A designer of bridges, tunnels and the Great Western Railway, Brunel also revolutionised shipbuilding. His SS *Great Britain*, launched in 1843, was the first ocean-going iron ship – and the biggest ship ever built. His steamship the *Great Eastern* laid the first successful telegraph cable under the Atlantic in 1866. Many people think of Brunel as Britain's greatest engineer.

My name is Brunel. I'm going to build the biggest ship in the world!

Designed as a luxury passenger ship, the SS Great Britain could carry 252 passengers and 130 crew.

SS GREAT BRITAIN

In 2002, Brunel came second in a BBC vote for the '100 Greatest Britons'. Winston Churchill got the top spot.

The people of Portsmouth should be extremely proud of Mr Brunel.

SPOT THIS!

This plaque in Britain Street marks Brunel's birthplace. Have you seen the real thing?

IN THIS STREET WAS BORN ON THE 9TH APRIL 1806 ISAMBARD KINGDOM BRUNEL THE GREAT ENGINEER

Riot!

In 1874, some people were seen bathing naked at Southsea Common. Most Victorians would have been very embarrassed by this and when the town council heard about it, they were angry. To stop it from happening again, the council decided to block people from getting to the Common. Led by a councillor called Barney Miller, the people of Portsmouth revolted and broke down the barricades. After four days of fighting, the Mayor read the Riot Act and the public won – they were free to use the park again.

In the Workhouse

The workhouse is hot and noisy. The workers are only there because it's the last option for their families – it's that or the streets. A 9-year-old girl shows her younger sister how to separate rope into fibres that will be sold to shipbuilders. The girls' skirts are made from coarse, itchy wool and are too long in the hope they will grow into them. Heavy, hobnailed shoes with iron tips rub blisters on the girls' toes. The workhouse master shouts at the children to work harder. Some of the younger children groan but the older ones know better.

> Mama said there was no room for me to live at home any more.

Poor Portsmouth

There were two Portsmouths during Victorian times. One was a wealthy, bustling, holiday town. The other was full of people who were desperately poor, couldn't read or write, and died young of poverty and disease. Children who had been abandoned or orphaned would roam the filthy streets around the Dockyard. They begged and stole food, sleeping wherever they could, in courtyards, alleys or even pigsties.

If children were naughty, they could be sent to prison. Others were given hard work as a punishment, like one 13-year-old boy who was caught stealing ginger beer and tobacco. In the first half of the 19th century, some children were even shipped off to Australia! In the mid-19th century, a fifth of Portsmouth children died before they were one year old — many more than the national average.

Rats!

Infected sailors brought all kinds of diseases back with them when ships returned to dock. Smallpox, cholera and typhus were all common in the poorer parts around the Dockyard. Rats that had lived onboard the ships also spread disease as they scurried off onto the streets of Portsmouth.

...1860 ROYAL MARINE BARRACKS BUILT IN PORTSMOUTH...

Nicholas Nickleby

Charles John Huffam Dickens was born in Portsmouth in 1812. Dickens wrote many novels describing the life of the poor in Victorian England. For a short time, he lived near his father's place of work in the Dockyard pay office, before moving to what is now King's Road. His memories of Portsmouth are not happy ones. He said that Portsmouth was 'remarkable for mud...and sailors'.

Charles Dickens didn't have many happy memories of Portsmouth.

Arthur Conan Doyle was living in Portsmouth when he wrote his first Sherlock Holmes novel.

Dickens' birthplace is now a museum, furnished in the style of the early 1800s.

My favourite Dickens novel is *A Christmas Carol*. Poor Tiny Tim!

Dickens set the serial novel *Nicholas Nickleby* in his hometown. The main character, Nicholas, finds himself 'among bare walls, dusty scenes... and dirty floors...all looked coarse, cold, gloomy and wretched'. Despite their poor surroundings, Dickens' characters are often upbeat and hopeful. His most well-loved characters include Oliver Twist, the Artful Dodger and Tiny Tim.

CHARLES DICKENS WAS BORN IN THIS HOUSE ON 7TH FEBRUARY 1812

This plaque was placed here by the Portsmouth Branch of the Dickens Fellowship in May 1978

SPOT THIS!

If you go to the house where Charles Dickens was born, you'll find this plaque outside.

Before the 1870 Education Act, many children in Portsmouth did not go to school. The main schools in Portsmouth were the Grammar School, which opened in 1750, and the 'Old Benny', set up by the Beneficial Society. In 1818 a shoe mender called John Pounds set up a free school for poor children in his cramped workshop.

By 1880, the law said that children had to go to school between the ages of 5 and 10. At 7 years old, girls and boys were separated and playgrounds were walled off. Here is an imaginary account of school by 10-year-old Emily Benyon.

The 'Old Benny' school used this building in Kent Street, Portsea. It was originally set up in 1755.

The first school in Portsmouth was only for boys. Girls weren't allowed to go!

Today felt like a long day at school. In the morning, we had scripture, drill, geography and sums. Geography is my favourite subject, though I doubt I will ever visit any of the places we learn about.

At break we play tag, hopscotch, tops, skipping and hoops. The boys play marbles and conkers. I look forward to Tuesday mornings the most, when about a dozen of us go to cookery classes at Drayton Road. The boys do woodwork and metalwork.

Afternoons are for needlework. We get on with our sewing while a girl reads to us. We also do history and singing. Our teacher has an awful singing voice and makes me want to cover my ears!

When I finish school, my first job will be in the nearby vicarage as a between-maid. I will get up at 6 o'clock every morning, say my morning prayers and work all day long. My only day off will be the first day of every month. I hope the vicar and his wife are not too strict...

UDOR 1485-1603

STUART 1603-1714

GEORGIAN 1714-1837

VICTORIAN 1837-1901

MODERN TIMES
1902-NOW

Listen, children! If you do not pay attention, I shall have you shipped off to Australia with the convicts!

This is a life-sized model of John Pounds' workshop. He taught the children everything he knew – how to cook, read, write and mend shoes. After John Pounds died, his idea of free schools for poor or 'ragged' children spread throughout the country. They were known as 'Ragged Schools'.

The John Pounds Memorial Church contains this monument.

How do we know?

Much of Victorian Portsmouth is still there today, including the piers and railway station.
The building used by Portsmouth Beneficial School, or the 'Old Benny', still stands in Kent Street, Portsea, and a life-sized model of John Pounds' workshop stands in the gardens of the John Pounds Memorial Church. His original school was based in what is now Highbury Street.
Novels, diaries, postcards and letters all tell us about Victorian life. One letter in 'The Portsmouth Papers' is written by John Kingswell, who went to the Old Benny School from 1836 to 1838. He described the school as 'dark, dingy, cold and miserable'. Kingswell left school when he was 11 years old and entered the dockyard as an apprentice shipwright.

Portsmouth at War

The navy is about to set sail from Portsmouth Harbour. It's time to say goodbye to Fred and Bertie and all the other sons, brothers and fathers in their crisp new uniforms. Women wave their handkerchiefs, trying not to cry. Little children wave too, but they don't really understand what is happening. The sailors are excited but nervous – they don't know when, or if, they will come home. They put on brave faces and wave back, then turn to join the hoards of men boarding the battleships.

Working Women

When men went off to war in 1914, women took their places in the Dockyard. The men who still worked there often taunted them. One woman recalled the need for an umbrella 'to give as much as you received'. Working women faced another problem. They could make shells and guns, be doctors and nurses, teachers and mayors. But they could not vote.

Some Portsmouth women joined the 'Votes for Women' movement. They included Nora O'Shea, 'the red-haired rebel', and her sister Margaret, who wrote the powerful words to the suffragette song, 'Forward, Ever Forward'. Women had to wait until 1928 to gain the right to vote on equal terms with men.

Forward, ever forward, ladies! We mustn't stop until we get the vote!

VOTES FOR WOMEN

Hertha Ayrton was one woman from Portsmouth who contributed to the war effort in a different way. Born in Portsea, Hertha became an engineer, mathematician and inventor. Although Hertha passed her maths degree at Cambridge University, she was not awarded it – women at that time were not allowed to receive degrees. Hertha invented a number of devices, including the Ayrton Anti-Gas Fan, which was used to send poison gas away from the trenches in World War One.

TUDOR 1485-1603	STUART 1603-1714	GEORGIAN 1714-1837	VICTORIAN 1837-1901	MODERN TIMES 1902-NOW

Air Raids

During World War Two, the Germans made 67 air raids on Portsmouth. They dropped 1,320 high explosives, 380,000 fire bombs and 38 land mines. About 930 civilians were killed. More families were broken up as men went off to war. Over half of factory workers were now women, and the first female Lord Mayor was appointed. Many children were evacuated and went to live in the countryside, away from the bombing.

SPOT THIS!

This church lost its roof when it was hit by a German bomb. Do you know whereabouts it is in Portsmouth?

Corporal Welch kept a diary of events during the war. His notes mention that Clarence Pier was destroyed, along with the Guildhall, the hospital and some churches.

Corporal John Welch was based in Portsmouth in 1941. His uncle was a colonel in Portsmouth.

D-Day Landings

Portsmouth sent all kinds of ships, from ferryboats to fishing smacks, across the English Channel to rescue troops retreating from Dunkirk in 1940. Two years later, Royal Marines – the 'Cockleshell Heroes' – set off from Eastney beach to attack German ships in Bordeaux.

June 1944 was an important time for Portsmouth. Three Allied commanders used Southwick House, a mansion near Portsmouth, as their headquarters to plan a massive attack on Germany. Allied troops would land on the beaches of Normandy, in France, to drive the Germans back from the coast.

Nearly 27,000 troops and 4,200 vehicles were loaded onto 290 landing craft. They crossed the Channel from Portsmouth to Normandy. 6th June, when most of the attacks took place, became known as 'D-Day'.

On 8th May 1945, German forces in Europe surrendered and the people of Portsmouth celebrated with fancy dress and street parties.

...1944 ALLIED TROOPS LAUNCH FROM PORTSMOUTH FOR D-DAY LANDINGS...

27

Portsmouth Today and Tomorrow...

After the war, there was a lot of patching up to do in Portsmouth. The people were determined to rebuild a better city, while protecting its proud heritage. The city moved with the times. Many churches, cinemas and theatres shut down and HMS *Vernon* became a shopping centre. Much of the Dockyard became a museum, and new structures and shops were built, attracting thousands of people to Portsmouth.

Launched in 1860, HMS *Warrior* was the most powerful ship of her day. Step onboard to find out about life as a Victorian sailor. Could it inspire future generations to join the navy?

The cannon and guns on HMS *Warrior* are amazing! I joined in with a gun drill!

The Blue Reef Aquarium® sits between the two piers in Portsmouth. There's a giant ocean tank and an underwater tunnel to make you feel like you're walking right along the seabed. Watch out for the pufferfish!

A spinnaker sail catches the wind by billowing out in front of the boat. Can you see how the tower got its name?

At 170 metres in height, the Spinnaker Tower is the tallest structure in the UK, outside of London. It gives amazing views of the harbour and has Europe's biggest glass floor. Are you brave enough to step onto it?

...1982 MARY ROSE RAISED FROM SOLENT...2005 SPINNAKER TOWER BUILT...

The hull of the Mary Rose will be on display from 2012, as part of a new museum in Portsmouth. The museum aims to show how life on a Tudor warship would have been, with all its noise and chaos!

Gunwharf Quays is a big shopping centre on the waterfront in Portsmouth. As well as shops and restaurants, there is a cinema, gym and bowling alley. Plenty for you to do!

SPOT THIS!

This statue was unveiled in 1997, in memory of the soldiers who died in World War Two. Do you know where it is?

How will they know?

We know about the history of Portsmouth from what people have left behind. Newspapers, articles and photographs all provide evidence of the past 100 years or more. Tourists visit and take photos to show family and friends. But with digital cameras and the Internet, a lot of our evidence is now electronic. Will there be enough proof of today's Portsmouth to show people in 100 years' time? What about 1,000 years' time? Historic ships have been docked at Portsmouth for generations of people to see and explore. How much longer will they stay there? What about the vehicles we use today – will they be around in 500 years' time, like the Mary Rose?

Portsmouth's D-Day Museum has tanks, uniforms, a film show and lots more. Do you think museums in the future will tell people about our troops today?

29

Glossary

Abbey – a building where monks or nuns live and work.

Accessory – a small item that can be worn, such as a brooch or hairpin.

AD – a short way of writing the Latin words anno Domini, which mean 'in the year of our Lord', i.e. after the birth of Christ.

Apprentice – a person who is learning a trade.

Artefact – another word for an object, often with archaeological or historical meaning.

Barracks – a building or place where soldiers stay.

Charter – royal permission.

Cholera – a deadly disease caused by filthy water.

Christian – a member of the Christian religion, which follows the teachings of Christ.

Christianity – the Christian religion, which believes Christ is the son of God.

Domesday Survey – William the Conqueror wanted to know how much land and money there was in his Kingdom. So he sent his men all over England to check what everyone owned. The results of this survey were written in a book called the Domesday Book.

Galley ship – a ship rowed by slaves and used to transport goods.

Harbour – where boats can dock safely and be tied up.

Jester – a kind of clown who entertained people.

Legion – a military unit of between 3,000 and 6,000 men in the Roman army.

Legionaries – soldiers belonging to the Roman Legion.

Minstrel – a musician who travelled around the country entertaining people for money.

Monastery – a place where monks live and worship.

Pagan – someone who believes in lots of different gods rather than just one.

Runes – an ancient alphabet believed to be magical.

Shipwright – someone who has learned how to build ships.

Slaves – any person who is owned by another. Slaves have no rights or freedom and work for no payment.

Suffragette – a woman who believed that women had the right to vote and was prepared to fight for this right.

Thane – a person of rank, often of the nobility or upper class.

Treadmill – a basic kind of machine, like a wheel, which works if a person or animal walks inside to make it turn and produce energy.

Turnspit – a bar across a fire on which animals were hung, so they could be cooked.

Typhus – an infectious disease that causes fever and sometimes death.

Vectis – the Roman name for the Isle of Wight.

Workhouse – where poor people lived and worked, when they had nowhere else to go.

Ynys-Wyth – another name for the Isle of Wight, meaning 'channel island'.

…HELEN DUNCAN, LAST WOMAN TO BE CHARGED AS A WITCH, LIVED IN PORTSMOUTH.

Index

Acknowledgements

The author and publishers would like to thank the following people for their generous help:
Emma Clarke-Bolton at Sarah Eastel Locations; Chris Medlock, for all her assistance at the Fishbourne Museum;
Dr Dominic Fontana FRG, Department of Geography, University of Portsmouth, and Kester Keighley for kindly
agreeing to the use of the Mary Rose Cowdray engraving; Sally Tyrrell for her greatly appreciated help at the Mary Rose
Museum; Penelope Welch for her very kind assistance and for allowing the use of her father's pictures.

The publishers would like to thank the following people and organisations
for their permission to reproduce material on the following pages:
Front cover: The Royal Naval museum; p4: English Heritage; p5: Classical Numismatic Group, Inc.
www.cngcoins.com, English Heritage; p6 and p7: Fishbourne Museum; p8: Bodleian Library, University of Oxford,
MS. Laud. Misc. 636, fol. 1r; p9: Hampshire County Council Museums Service; p10: www.historymedren.about.com;
p11: Diane Earl, English Heritage; p13: Werner Forman Archive; p16: The Mary Rose Trust, engraving by kind permission
of Kester Keighley; p17: The Mary Rose Trust; p18: Image Courtesy of Heritage Auction Galleries, ha.com; p20: Old UK
Photos; p27: Family archives of John Marsh Welch of Dunmow, Essex; p29: Wilkinson Eyre Architects.

Written by Jim Riordan
Educational consultant: Neil Thompson
Local history consultant: Tim Lambert
Designed by Stephen Prosser

Illustrated by Tim Hutchinson, Kate Davies, Peter Kent and John MacGregor
Additional photographs by Alex Long

First published by HOMETOWN WORLD in 2010
Hometown World Ltd
7 Northumberland Buildings
Bath BA1 2JB

www.hometownworld.co.uk

Copyright © Hometown World Ltd 2010

ISBN 978-1-84993-005-5
All rights reserved
Printed in China

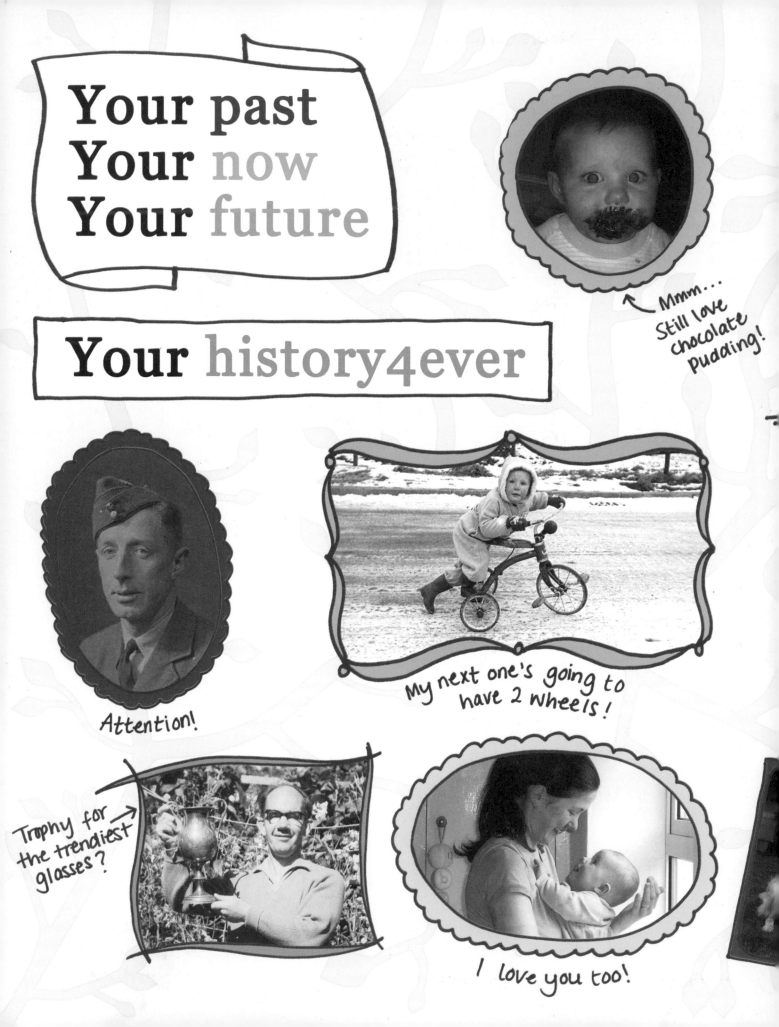

Your past
Your now
Your future

Your history4ever

Mmm... Still love chocolate pudding!

Attention!

My next one's going to have 2 wheels!

Trophy for the trendiest glasses?

I love you too!